LITTLE WHITE BOOK

Gratitude

Part I

ALICIA WADE

BALBOA.PRESS
A DIVISION OF HAY HOUSE

Gratitude

Balboa Press books may be ordered through booksellers or by contacting:

Balboa Press
A Division of Hay House
1663 Liberty Drive
Bloomington, IN 47403
www.balboapress.com.au
AU TFN: 1 800 844 925 (Toll Free inside Australia)
AU Local: 0283 107 086 (+61 2 8310 7086 from outside Australia)

Print information available on the last page.

ISBN: 978-1-5043-2412-0 (sc)
ISBN: 978-1-5043-2414-4 (hc)
ISBN: 978-1-5043-2413-7 (e)

Balboa Press rev. date: 04/07/2021

About Alicia Ann Wade

Alicia is a Gratitude Expert, Coach, Business Mentor, Motivational Speaker, and Author. She has worked in Early Childhood Education, been a TAFE teacher, a trainer and a facilitator. A Community Leader for Be You for Beyond Blue, and a Big Steps Campaign Leader in her town of Hervey Bay for Early Childhood Education.

She has also been awarded one of the highest awards in TAFE for Innovation in the workplace 2002, Early Childhood Educator of the year 2013, Centre of the Year 2013, 2015 & 2016 and recently International Life Coach of the Year 2020.

She is on a mission to help and assist others with Depression, Anxiety and Mental Health. She has had her own battles and successes throughout her life. She was teased as a child for her weight, failed the school system, couldn't read or understand English, failed university, has overcome dysfunction relationships to have more meaning driven relationships, took many party drugs & abused alcohol and overcame a depressive state of mind. She understood the commitment, dedication, and self-love and effort that were required to turn her life around.

About Alicia Ann Wade

Gratitude is one of those improvements and rituals she has incorporated to her life.

Alicia will take you on a journey of self-empowerment, direction, and control in life. This is the fourth edition of this book, it was originally made on Christmas Day 2018. It has transformed just like Alicia has over the years. This book started off as spiral bound, to soft cover & now to hard cover.

Over the last couple of years, Alicia has heard people use this journal as a way to stay here on earth and bring gratitude to their world, the power of Gratitude is like no other and so it is Alicia's mission to spread this far and wide.

Her goal is 1 million lives! Let's help her achieve this!

Gratitude is the best attitude!

Gratitude

Let's begin your 52 week Gratitude Challenge

Firstly, Thank you for taking the time to purchase this 52 week challenge. I have created this with all the tools and resources I have collected from many people. I realised I have so much to offer, and so much to give, and so much to share.

So, it is only fair to start giving support to others around the world. My mission is to spread gratitude to over 1 million people, a huge goal but one which I hope to smash out of the park.

I have seen people completely change their worlds from adding Gratitude to their life.

When we scratch the record of negativity you start to enter a world of positivity. I have to firstly say, "Thank you" to Tayla Davis who pushed me over and over again to write this and get this done!

I needed a little shove and push to get this out and I am finally getting this done for my people far and wide and spreading acts of kindness everywhere.

So, this challenge will have a weekly task to action and also some activities to do over the course of 52 weeks.

I thought it would be really effective if we added some activities too that I have gained from a variety of people that I have learnt from in my world and now for you to add in your world!

So, let the games begin and get you kick started on your Gratitude journey. I look forward to what will occur and let this really ramp it up with positivity.

After you complete this book, please share, like and review what happened for you. Spread this! With today's society, COVID,
Loss, depression, mental health, suicide, anxiety
ETC ETC ETC ETC
We need to start making changes and spreading this around! It is the natural way of being and doing! Trust me! It works! I've had many messages to say how gratitude has saved lives and people have stayed on earth from a simple practice. The POWER of this is phenomenal.

Enjoy this book! Like I did creating this.

With love, light, gratitude and thanks,
Alicia Ann Wade

Week 1 Challenge

NATURE:

Take a walk in nature, look, listen and feel your surroundings. It is time to go out in nature and feel, hear and see what mother nature has to offer. Whether you get out once or all 7 days. Get out of the house and into nature.

Doing What You Want

What did you want to do at home? At work? Anywhere else? With yourself?
Did you do it? If not, why not?

_____

_____

_____

_____

_____

_____

Did you ever not know what you wanted to do? If yes, why was that? What did you do to
resolve your uncertainty / confusion?

_____

_____

_____

_____

_____

_____

What patterns do you notice?

_____

_____

_____

_____

_____

_____

Your past does not define your future

Daily Gratitude

DATE:

I am grateful for:

_____

_____

_____

_____

_____

_____

_____

_____

_____

_____

_____

_____

_____

_____

_____

_____

_____

_____

Daily Affirmation about myself

I AM:

Happiness Scale % :

0   25   50   75   100

Great minds discuss ideas, average minds discuss events, small minds discuss people. Eleanor Roosevelt

Daily Gratitude

DATE:

I am grateful for:

_____

_____

_____

_____

_____

_____

_____

_____

_____

_____

_____

_____

_____

_____

_____

_____

_____

Daily Affirmation about myself

I AM:

Happiness Scale % :

0	25	50	75	100

#gratitudeisthebestattitude

Daily Gratitude

DATE:

I am grateful for:

_____

_____

_____

_____

_____

_____

_____

_____

_____

_____

_____

_____

_____

_____

_____

_____

_____

_____

_____

_____

_____

Daily Affirmation about myself

I AM:

Happiness Scale % :

0   25   50   75   100

Daily Gratitude

DATE:

I am grateful for:

_____

_____

_____

_____

_____

_____

_____

_____

_____

_____

_____

_____

_____

_____

_____

_____

_____

_____

Daily Affirmation about myself

I AM:

Happiness Scale % :

0   25   50   75   100

Daily Gratitude

DATE:

I am grateful for:

_____
_____
_____
_____
_____
_____
_____
_____
_____
_____
_____
_____
_____
_____
_____
_____
_____
_____
_____
_____
_____
_____
_____
_____

Daily Affirmation about myself
I AM:

Happiness Scale % :

0   25   50   75   100

Be happy with the skin you are in

Daily Gratitude

DATE:

I am grateful for:

_____

_____

_____

_____

_____

_____

_____

_____

_____

_____

_____

_____

_____

_____

_____

_____

_____

_____

_____

Daily Affirmation about myself

I AM:

Happiness Scale % :

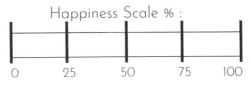

0   25   50   75   100

Strangers think I'm quiet, my friends think I'm outgoing, my best friends know I'm insane!

Daily Gratitude

DATE:

I am grateful for:

_____

_____

_____

_____

_____

_____

_____

_____

_____

_____

_____

_____

_____

_____

_____

_____

_____

_____

Daily Affirmation about myself

I AM:

Happiness Scale % :

0   25   50   75   100

Date:

Weekly Reflection

WEEK 1

Write about the 1st week of gratitude and reflect on what you noticed, felt, heard, saw and any other things you may of noticed.

_____

_____

_____

_____

_____

_____

_____

_____

_____

_____

_____

_____

_____

_____

_____

_____

_____

_____

_____

_____

_____

_____

_____

_____

_____

_____

_____

#gratitudeisthebestattitude

"Good morning is not just a word. It's an action and a belief to live the entire day well. Morning is the time when you set the tone for the rest of the day."
Fain Blake

Week 2 Challenge

TRANSPORT:

Appreciate how you go from point A to point B in your travelling in the day. Take the time over the week to notice how you are travelling to and from p laces. Bus, train, bike, car, truck, whatever is your means of transport. Take notice.

Wheel of Life!

This little tool is a gateway into ways in wanting to achieve the life we want to achieve. We need to be truly open and honest with ourselves if we want to go ahead in life and live a life on our terms and the path we want to lead. This will give insights on how you can be the best you can be by giving insights to where in your life you want to improve to gain the results you want to. When we are prepared and honest with ourselves, we can then go onto creating a plan of action to take the steps towards what it is you are wanting to achieve. The centre of the pie is a 0 if you are not achieving the different areas of your life. And the outer edge is a 10 if are achieving this or a little less. So take the time to rate yourself in each area and see what comes up for you. You may be surprised at what comes up for you. For example, Adventure is not where you want it to be and you are doing things but want to do more so you rate yourself in the middle.

Take the time to do this as you can create goals for next year on what you would like to focus on. You second last day you are creating a vision board so this wheel will assist in what you can create.

Have fun!

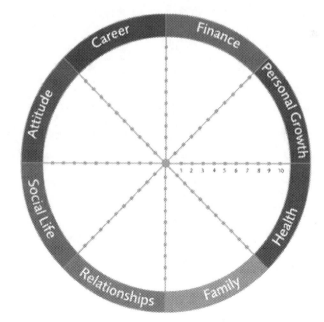

Daily Gratitude

DATE:

I am grateful for:

_____

_____

_____

_____

_____

_____

_____

_____

_____

_____

_____

_____

_____

_____

_____

_____

_____

_____

Daily Affirmation about myself

I AM:

Happiness Scale % :

0   25   50   75   100

You will get better with age as long as you let go of the past and let your joy lead the way

Daily Gratitude

DATE:

I am grateful for:

_____

_____

_____

_____

_____

_____

_____

_____

_____

_____

_____

_____

_____

_____

_____

_____

_____

_____

Daily Affirmation about myself
I AM:

Happiness Scale % :

0   25   50   75   100

You have to be ODD to be number 1 - Dr Seuss

Daily Gratitude

DATE:

I am grateful for:

_____

_____

_____

_____

_____

_____

_____

_____

_____

_____

_____

_____

_____

_____

_____

_____

_____

_____

Daily Affirmation about myself

I AM:

Happiness Scale % :

0   25   50   75   100

The best is yet to come, be patient

Daily Gratitude

DATE:

I am grateful for:

_____

_____

_____

_____

_____

_____

_____

_____

_____

_____

_____

_____

_____

_____

_____

_____

_____

_____

_____

Daily Affirmation about myself
I AM:

Happiness Scale % :

0   25   50   75   100

There are so many beautiful reasons to be happy.

Daily Gratitude

DATE:

I am grateful for:

_____

_____

_____

_____

_____

_____

_____

_____

_____

_____

_____

_____

_____

_____

_____

_____

_____

_____

_____

_____

Daily Affirmation about myself

I AM:

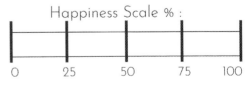

Happiness Scale % :

0   25   50   75   100

When it rains look for the rainbows, when it is dark look for the stars - Oscar Wilde

Daily Gratitude

D A T E :

I am grateful for:

_____

_____

_____

_____

_____

_____

_____

_____

_____

_____

_____

_____

_____

_____

_____

_____

_____

_____

_____

_____

Daily Affirmation about myself

I AM:

Happiness Scale % :

0   25   50   75   100

The future belongs to those who believe in their dreams. Eleanor Roosevelt

Daily Gratitude

DATE :

I am grateful for:

_____

_____

_____

_____

_____

_____

_____

_____

_____

_____

_____

_____

_____

_____

_____

_____

_____

_____

_____

Daily Affirmation about myself

I AM:

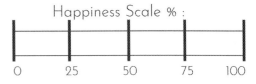

Happiness Scale % :

0   25   50   75   100

Date:

Weekly Reflection

Write about the 2nd week of gratitude and reflect on what you noticed, felt, heard, saw and any other things you may of noticed.

_____

_____

_____

_____

_____

_____

_____

_____

_____

_____

_____

_____

_____

_____

_____

_____

_____

_____

_____

_____

_____

_____

"Every dream begins with a dreamer. Always remember, you have within you the strength, the patience, and the passion to reach for the stars to change the world."
Harriet Tubman

Week 3 Challenge

ART:

Spend some time creating something or appreciating art or getting a friend involved. When we tap into creativity our minds wander and we learn more things about ourselves and drift off into creativity land. Let your mind wander.

What is important to do this week?

What new people did you open yourself to this week? How did that feel?

_____

_____

_____

_____

What new experiences did you have this week?

_____

_____

_____

_____

What was fun for you this week?

_____

_____

_____

_____

Whom did you inspire this week?

_____

_____

_____

_____

Positive mind. Positive vibes. Positive life

Daily Gratitude

DATE:

I am grateful for:

_____

_____

_____

_____

_____

_____

_____

_____

_____

_____

_____

_____

_____

_____

_____

_____

_____

_____

_____

_____

_____

Daily Affirmation about myself

I AM:

Happiness Scale % :

0   25   50   75   100

Life is good because I decided to make it that way - Anaah

Daily Gratitude

DATE:

I am grateful for:

_____

_____

_____

_____

_____

_____

_____

_____

_____

_____

_____

_____

_____

_____

_____

_____

_____

_____

_____

_____

Daily Affirmation about myself
I AM:

Happiness Scale % :

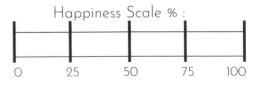

0   25   50   75   100

People be like, "why are you in such a good mood?" Because I can be!

Daily Gratitude

DATE:

I am grateful for:

_____

_____

_____

_____

_____

_____

_____

_____

_____

_____

_____

_____

_____

_____

_____

_____

_____

_____

Daily Affirmation about myself

I AM:

Happiness Scale % :

0   25   50   75   100

You can never expect to succeed if you only put in work on the days you feel like it

Daily Gratitude

DATE:

I am grateful for:

_____

_____

_____

_____

_____

_____

_____

_____

_____

_____

_____

_____

_____

_____

_____

_____

_____

Daily Affirmation about myself

I AM:

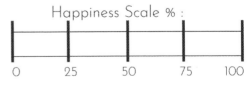

Happiness Scale % :

0   25   50   75   100

One day at a time....

Daily Gratitude

DATE:

I am grateful for:

_____

_____

_____

_____

_____

_____

_____

_____

_____

_____

_____

_____

_____

_____

_____

_____

_____

_____

Daily Affirmation about myself
I AM:

Happiness Scale % :

0   25   50   75   100

Believe in your dreams

Daily Gratitude

DATE:

I am grateful for:

_____

_____

_____

_____

_____

_____

_____

_____

_____

_____

_____

_____

_____

_____

_____

_____

_____

_____

_____

Daily Affirmation about myself
I AM:

Happiness Scale % :

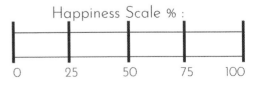

0   25   50   75   100

Be happy for this moment, this moment is your life

Daily Gratitude

DATE:

I am grateful for:

_____

_____

_____

_____

_____

_____

_____

_____

_____

_____

_____

_____

_____

_____

_____

_____

_____

_____

Daily Affirmation about myself
I AM:

Happiness Scale % :

0   25   50   75   100

Date:

Weekly Reflection

WEEK 3

Write about the 3rd week of gratitude and reflect on what you noticed, felt, heard,
saw and any other things you may of noticed.

_____

_____

_____

_____

_____

_____

_____

_____

_____

_____

_____

_____

_____

_____

_____

_____

_____

_____

_____

_____

_____

_____

_____

"It is easy to sit up and take notice. What is difficult is getting up and taking action."
Al Batt

Week 4 Challenge

MEDITATE:

Spend some time meditating for at least 10mins. See what happens to you mentally and watch your world change for the better when you incorporate this into your world!

What are your top goals for this challenge?

_____

_____

_____

_____

_____

_____

_____

What are your top goals for the year ahead?

_____

_____

_____

_____

_____

_____

_____

What are your top goals for the next 3 years?

_____

_____

_____

_____

_____

_____

_____

You should set goals beyond your reach so you always have something to live for. Ted Turner

Daily Gratitude

DATE:

I am grateful for:

_____

_____

_____

_____

_____

_____

_____

_____

_____

_____

_____

_____

_____

_____

_____

_____

_____

_____

Daily Affirmation about myself

I AM:

Happiness Scale % :

0   25   50   75   100

I know everything happens for a reason

Daily Gratitude

DATE:

I am grateful for:

_____

_____

_____

_____

_____

_____

_____

_____

_____

_____

_____

_____

_____

_____

_____

_____

_____

_____

Daily Affirmation about myself

I AM:

Happiness Scale % :

0   25   50   75   100

DREAM - At least once a day, allow yourself the freedom to think and dream - Albert Einstein

Daily Gratitude

DATE:

I am grateful for:

_____

_____

_____

_____

_____

_____

_____

_____

_____

_____

_____

_____

_____

_____

_____

_____

_____

Daily Affirmation about myself

I AM:

Happiness Scale % :

0   25   50   75   100

It's not enough to be busy, s are the ants, The question is: What are you busy about? Henry David Thoreau

Daily Gratitude

DATE:

I am grateful for:

_____

_____

_____

_____

_____

_____

_____

_____

_____

_____

_____

_____

_____

_____

_____

_____

_____

_____

_____

_____

_____

Daily Affirmation about myself

I AM:

Happiness Scale % :

0   25   50   75   100

This year: I will be stronger, braver, kinder & unstoppable. This year I will be fierce.

Daily Gratitude

DATE:

I am grateful for:

_____

_____

_____

_____

_____

_____

_____

_____

_____

_____

_____

_____

_____

_____

_____

_____

_____

Daily Affirmation about myself
I AM:

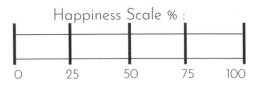

Happiness Scale % :

| 0 | 25 | 50 | 75 | 100 |

Don't worry about those who talk behind your back, they're behind your back for a reason...

Daily Gratitude

DATE:

I am grateful for:

_____

_____

_____

_____

_____

_____

_____

_____

_____

_____

_____

_____

_____

_____

_____

_____

_____

_____

_____

Daily Affirmation about myself

I AM:

Happiness Scale % :

0   25   50   75   100

You can't live a positive life with a negative mind

Daily Gratitude

DATE:

I am grateful for:

_____

_____

_____

_____

_____

_____

_____

_____

_____

_____

_____

_____

_____

_____

_____

_____

Daily Affirmation about myself
I AM:

Happiness Scale % :

0   25   50   75   100

Date:

Weekly Reflection

Write about the 4th week of gratitude and reflect on what you noticed, felt, heard, saw and any other things you may of noticed.

_____
_____
_____
_____
_____
_____
_____
_____
_____
_____
_____
_____
_____
_____
_____
_____
_____
_____
_____
_____
_____
_____
_____
_____
_____
_____
_____
_____

"Never give up, for that is just the place and time that the tide will turn."

Harriet Beecher Stowe

Week 5 Challenge

BE KIND:

Do a random act of kindness e.g. give a compliment to someone. Take note of how you feel inside when you do this for another person. Take the time out to be kind to others.

Living Healthy and Well

Now get a piece of paper
What unhealthy habits do you want to change?
WRITE THIS DOWN
Now write the opposite of what you have written on the blank page here:

_____

_____

_____

_____

_____

_____

_____

_____

_____

_____

_____

Now, it is time to go and burn or rip up the unhealthy habits. It is not serving you anymore, there should be a time and a place to burn this safely or rip the paper up into shreds. Watch the paper burn and feel the emotions or rip the paper up and feel into those feelings.

Feel the feelings you feel that come up for you, Cry if you need to, Be happy, Be empowered. Whatever feelings come up, embrace this as this is the transformational time and the experience you are needing right now for yourself. Trust this process and this time to discover who you need to be in the world and who you want to show up as. Create your new mantra, place it in a place where you can see it, where you can remind yourself. You can scratch the record of old thoughts and discover your true potential.

I would even suggest having something on the mirror. Look into your eyes and tell it to yourself! Say it out loud and proud! You deserve this! You are beautiful! BIG HUGS!

Daily Gratitude

DATE:

I am grateful for:

_____

_____

_____

_____

_____

_____

_____

_____

_____

_____

_____

_____

_____

_____

_____

_____

_____

_____

_____

_____

Daily Affirmation about myself

I AM:

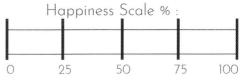

Happiness Scale % :

0   25   50   75   100

Happiness and good vibes are contagious. Help spread them

Daily Gratitude

DATE:

I am grateful for:

_____

_____

_____

_____

_____

_____

_____

_____

_____

_____

_____

_____

_____

_____

_____

_____

_____

_____

_____

_____

Daily Affirmation about myself
I AM:

Happiness Scale % :

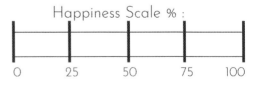

0   25   50   75   100

Don't wait. The time will never be right. - Napoleon Hill

Daily Gratitude

DATE:

I am grateful for:

_____

_____

_____

_____

_____

_____

_____

_____

_____

_____

_____

_____

_____

_____

_____

_____

_____

_____

_____

_____

_____

Daily Affirmation about myself

I AM:

Happiness Scale % :

0   25   50   75   100

When you can't find the sunshine, be the sunshine

Daily Gratitude

DATE:

I am grateful for:

_____

_____

_____

_____

_____

_____

_____

_____

_____

_____

_____

_____

_____

_____

_____

_____

_____

Daily Affirmation about myself
I AM:

Happiness Scale % :

0   25   50   75   100

Setting goals is the first step in turning the invisible into the visible
- Tony Robbins

Daily Gratitude

DATE:

I am grateful for:

_____

_____

_____

_____

_____

_____

_____

_____

_____

_____

_____

_____

_____

_____

_____

_____

_____

_____

_____

_____

Daily Affirmation about myself
I AM:

Happiness Scale % :

0   25   50   75   100

What is life without a little bit of risk? Sirus Black

Daily Gratitude

I am grateful for:

_____

_____

_____

_____

_____

_____

_____

_____

_____

_____

_____

_____

_____

_____

_____

_____

_____

_____

Daily Affirmation about myself
I AM:

Happiness Scale % :

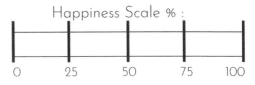

0   25   50   75   100

All of life is a journey. Which path we take, what we look back on, and what we look forward to is up to us!

Daily Gratitude

DATE:

I am grateful for:

_____

_____

_____

_____

_____

_____

_____

_____

_____

_____

_____

_____

_____

_____

_____

_____

_____

Daily Affirmation about myself
I AM:

Happiness Scale % :

0   25   50   75   100

Date:

Weekly Reflection

WEEK 5

Write about the 5th week of gratitude and reflect on what you noticed, felt, heard, saw and any other things you may of noticed.

_____

_____

_____

_____

_____

_____

_____

_____

_____

_____

_____

_____

_____

_____

_____

_____

_____

_____

_____

_____

_____

_____

_____

_____

"There's a future version of you who's proud of you were strong enough."

Week 6 Challenge

CONNECT:

Ring someone you haven't spoken to in a while and tell them what you are grateful for about them. There is nothing better than a phone to a friend or family member. So what are you waiting for pick up that phone and call someone.

Role Resignation

This is a chance to now get rid of the old role you played in life and bring in new elements of you! Get you pen and pad ready and it's time to get you to bring in new elements of you.

This is going to a great way to start fresh and set you on the path you want for health and wellness. It takes time to write it so go into a place where it is quiet and write this letter to yourself.

After you have written this letter, what I want you to do is keep it somewhere handy where you can read it over and over again, reminding you of who you are now becoming. It suits you the NEW you. You are no longer that old person, the old role you played. It's time. Enough is enough of playing the same old record.

Get that new record and play a new song to repeat. This is the new destiny you have longed for. When love creeps in nothing else really matters, especially when it is to yourself.

I,_____, am telling you, I am resigning from the role of the _____.

It has cost me time,

my people,

my _____,

my _____,

my _____,

my _____,

my _____,

my _____,

my _____,

I am going to learn to stop _____

and learn to _____

I am set to keep _____

I am keeping _____

I am going to practice_____

I am going to practice_____

Trust in the process of levelling up in the world.

Love ME!

The difference between TRY and TRIUMPH is a little UMP. - Marvin Phillips

Daily Gratitude

DATE:

I am grateful for:

_____

_____

_____

_____

_____

_____

_____

_____

_____

_____

_____

_____

_____

_____

_____

_____

_____

_____

Daily Affirmation about myself
I AM:

Happiness Scale % :

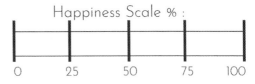

0   25   50   75   100

Daily Gratitude

DATE:

I am grateful for:

_____

_____

_____

_____

_____

_____

_____

_____

_____

_____

_____

_____

_____

_____

_____

_____

_____

_____

_____

_____

Daily Affirmation about myself
I AM:

Happiness Scale % :

0   25   50   75   100

Your success will bother some people. As will your enthusiasm, ambition and happiness. You'll survive. Craig Harper

Daily Gratitude

DATE:

I am grateful for:

_____

_____

_____

_____

_____

_____

_____

_____

_____

_____

_____

_____

_____

_____

_____

_____

_____

_____

Daily Affirmation about myself
I AM:

Happiness Scale % :

0   25   50   75   100

#gratitudeisthebestattitude

Change isn't by chance it's by choice. - Sharon Pearson

Daily Gratitude

DATE:

I am grateful for:

_____

_____

_____

_____

_____

_____

_____

_____

_____

_____

_____

_____

_____

_____

_____

_____

_____

_____

_____

Daily Affirmation about myself
I AM:

Happiness Scale % :

0   25   50   75   100

We must take the time to stop & thank the people who make a difference in our lives. John F. Kennedy

Daily Gratitude

DATE:

I am grateful for:

_____

_____

_____

_____

_____

_____

_____

_____

_____

_____

_____

_____

_____

_____

_____

_____

_____

_____

Daily Affirmation about myself

I AM:

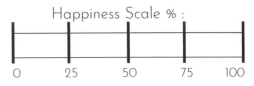

Happiness Scale % :

0   25   50   75   100

Never stop learning, because life never stops teaching

Daily Gratitude

DATE:

I am grateful for:

_____

_____

_____

_____

_____

_____

_____

_____

_____

_____

_____

_____

_____

_____

_____

_____

_____

Daily Affirmation about myself
I AM:

Happiness Scale % :

0   25   50   75   100

Do one thing everyday that scares you. Eleanor Roosevelt

Daily Gratitude

DATE:

I am grateful for:

_____

_____

_____

_____

_____

_____

_____

_____

_____

_____

_____

_____

_____

_____

_____

_____

_____

Daily Affirmation about myself
I AM:

Happiness Scale % :

0   25   50   75   100

Date:

Weekly Reflection

Write about the 6th week of gratitude and reflect on what you noticed, felt, heard, saw and any other things you may of noticed.

_____

_____

_____

_____

_____

_____

_____

_____

_____

_____

_____

_____

_____

_____

_____

_____

_____

_____

_____

_____

_____

_____

_____

_____

_____

_____

_____

_____

"Smile in the mirror. Do that every morning and you'll start to see a big difference in your life."
Yoko Ono

Week 7 Challenge

TOUCH:

Appreciate the power of a hug or holding hands with a loved one. Do it repetitively throughout the week an notice how your sense of wellbeing improves.

Know How You Feel

All over the world many people find it challenging to get in touch with emotions. Especially in this world when we are told to suck it up and get on with it. What does this do? suppress it further.

So, what is the activity going to consist of?

Well, what I want to do is for you to start naming your emotions and how they feel. We need to get in touch with these emotions and accompany the thoughts that go with it and make more meaning to it.

When we become more present to the emotions coming up we feel it, we name it, then we place a meaning on it. For example, your partner isn't meeting the need of connection for you and you feel isolated or lonely, you can share your experience honestly, letting them know what you need rather than behaving in an irritable or critical way.

Knowing exactly how you feel lets you have the chance to develop many different ways of how you choose to react and respond or manage the emotions you have. When you understand your own emotions, you will be a better place to recognise the way others are feeling and you'll have a greater capacity for empathy.

Time to do some activities now:

Take the time to close your eyes and become aware of your body parts that are relaxed, and the parts that are tight and uncomfortable. When you find a spot that is different or unique explore what it is. If you find a spot that is unusual, explore exactly how it feels. Is it physical, is it emotional? If there is a sign of an emotion give it a label and then let go. You will notice a shift in emotions as you let it go.

After naming this emotion and letting go, go ahead and ask yourself this: "Is there anything else I am feeling?" Emotions and feelings can be hard and they can be quiet complex, sometimes we hide behind a mask and there is much more underneath. Sometimes there is anger needed to come out, or maybe vulnerability or loneliness. These are universal feelings and it is empowering to recognise them for what they are coming up as and label then without judging yourself. It is ok to feel these feelings.

Be open and curious and open about all your feelings you have. It does take time to connect deeply with them. You may need support from a coach, or counsellor or psychologist.

Your future self will thank you for this

Daily Gratitude

DATE:

I am grateful for:

_____

_____

_____

_____

_____

_____

_____

_____

_____

_____

_____

_____

_____

_____

_____

_____

_____

_____

_____

Daily Affirmation about myself
I AM:

Happiness Scale % :

0   25   50   75   100

If you really want to catch your dreams, you have to chase it

Daily Gratitude

DATE:

I am grateful for:

_____

_____

_____

_____

_____

_____

_____

_____

_____

_____

_____

_____

_____

_____

_____

_____

_____

Daily Affirmation about myself

I AM:

Happiness Scale % :

0   25   50   75   100

Daily Gratitude

DATE:

I am grateful for:

_____

_____

_____

_____

_____

_____

_____

_____

_____

_____

_____

_____

_____

_____

_____

_____

_____

_____

_____

_____

_____

_____

Daily Affirmation about myself
I AM:

Happiness Scale % :

0   25   50   75   100

Repeat after me: "My current situation is not my final destination"

Daily Gratitude

DATE:

I am grateful for:

_____

_____

_____

_____

_____

_____

_____

_____

_____

_____

_____

_____

_____

_____

_____

_____

_____

Daily Affirmation about myself
I AM:

Happiness Scale % :

0   25   50   75   100

Commit yourself to lifelong learning. The most valuable asset you'll ever have is your mind and what you put into it. Brain Tracey.

Daily Gratitude

DATE:

I am grateful for:

_____

_____

_____

_____

_____

_____

_____

_____

_____

_____

_____

_____

_____

_____

_____

_____

_____

_____

_____

Daily Affirmation about myself

I AM:

Happiness Scale % :

0   25   50   75   100

Daily Gratitude

DATE:

I am grateful for:

_____

_____

_____

_____

_____

_____

_____

_____

_____

_____

_____

_____

_____

_____

_____

_____

_____

_____

_____

Daily Affirmation about myself
I AM:

Happiness Scale % :

0   25   50   75   100

You glow differently when you're actually happy

Daily Gratitude

DATE:

I am grateful for:

_____

_____

_____

_____

_____

_____

_____

_____

_____

_____

_____

_____

_____

_____

_____

_____

_____

_____

_____

Daily Affirmation about myself
I AM:

Happiness Scale % :

0   25   50   75   100

Date:

Weekly Reflection

WEEK 7

Write about the 7th week of gratitude and reflect on what you noticed, felt, heard, saw
and any other things you may of noticed.

_____

_____

_____

_____

_____

_____

_____

_____

_____

_____

_____

_____

_____

_____

_____

_____

_____

_____

_____

_____

_____

_____

_____

_____

_____

#gratitudeisthebestattitude

"Be so busy loving your life that you have no time for hate, regrets, or fear."

Karen Salmansohn

Week 8 Challenge

BUSINESS:

Support local! Go tell them you appreciate them! Our community need us to keep them thriving and being open. Without us they would not survive. So, go and support your local shops this week.

Enjoy Healthy Food

Food is one of the most important things we have to eat in order to live and a great pleasure in life. So, we need to ensure we eat mindfully. Sadly people develop an unhealthy relationship with food, they see food as the problem and issue. When really it is the mind. Eating consciously and mindfully will change the way you eat on a day to day basis.

All that is out there, it is no wonder we get confused of what is "right" and what is "wrong" and probably most of the information that is out there can contradict each other. I recommend that food is not the enemy, it is there to nourish your vessel and keep you alive!
Instead of having that constant head noise and guilt, choose the foods that are good for you and you will realise you will stop beating yourself up. Make sure you eat the right portions too.
Think of foods as "everyday foods" and "sometimes" foods to avoid being good or bad and scratch the record of negativity.

What you can do to ensure you eat more mindfully:

Find natural food you really like and start eating them regularly.

Start to really listen to your body and the hunger pains. Are you hungry or are you thirsty? Get in touch with your natural signs of hunger pains.

Be aware of when you start to emotionally eat! This can end up negative, you will beat yourself up, so instead be aware of the emotions and be softer on yourself. Emotionally eating can be hard. This challenge could help you with getting your mind off emotionally eating, so choose a activity on the calendar.

Make sure you are sitting down for every meal, ensure you are focused only on eating. Pay attention to the taste, the feelings and experience you are having.

Now is the time to start eating slowly. Chew well and place your knife and fork down when you are eating.

Stop eating when you feel 70% full as your body and mind take time to register when you are actually full.

One day or day one, You decide...

Daily Gratitude

DATE:

I am grateful for:

_____

_____

_____

_____

_____

_____

_____

_____

_____

_____

_____

_____

_____

_____

_____

_____

_____

_____

_____

Daily Affirmation about myself
I AM:

Happiness Scale % :

0   25   50   75   100

Keep it real or keep it moving...

Daily Gratitude

DATE:

I am grateful for:

_____

_____

_____

_____

_____

_____

_____

_____

_____

_____

_____

_____

_____

_____

_____

_____

_____

_____

_____

_____

Daily Affirmation about myself

I AM:

Happiness Scale % :

0   25   50   75   100

You will never change your life until you change something you do.
- John C. Maxwell

Daily Gratitude

DATE:

I am grateful for:

_____

_____

_____

_____

_____

_____

_____

_____

_____

_____

_____

_____

_____

_____

_____

_____

Daily Affirmation about myself
I AM:

Happiness Scale % :

0   25   50   75   100

There are two types of pains, one that hurts you and the other that changes you

Daily Gratitude

DATE:

I am grateful for:

_____

_____

_____

_____

_____

_____

_____

_____

_____

_____

_____

_____

_____

_____

_____

_____

_____

_____

Daily Affirmation about myself

I AM:

Happiness Scale % :

0   25   50   75   100

Your setback is the platform for your comeback

Daily Gratitude

DATE:

I am grateful for:

_____

_____

_____

_____

_____

_____

_____

_____

_____

_____

_____

_____

_____

_____

_____

_____

_____

_____

Daily Affirmation about myself
I AM:

Happiness Scale % :

0   25   50   75   100

True leaders don't create followers. They create more leaders. -
Tom Peters

Daily Gratitude

DATE:

I am grateful for:

_____

_____

_____

_____

_____

_____

_____

_____

_____

_____

_____

_____

_____

_____

_____

_____

_____

_____

_____

Daily Affirmation about myself
I AM:

Happiness Scale % :

0   25   50   75   100

Just play, have fun, enjoy the game. - Michael Jordan

Daily Gratitude

DATE:

I am grateful for:

_____

_____

_____

_____

_____

_____

_____

_____

_____

_____

_____

_____

_____

_____

_____

_____

_____

_____

Daily Affirmation about myself
I AM:

Happiness Scale % :

0   25   50   75   100

Date:

Weekly Reflection

WEEK 8

Write about the 8th week of gratitude and reflect on what you noticed, felt, heard, saw and any other things you may of noticed.

_____

_____

_____

_____

_____

_____

_____

_____

_____

_____

_____

_____

_____

_____

_____

_____

_____

_____

_____

_____

_____

_____

_____

_____

_____

_____

"Don't feel guilty for doing what's best for you."
Aditya Rai

Week 9 Challenge

WEATHER:

Give thanks to the weather and how much it changes from day to day. Every day we different sunrises and sunsets. Or cloudy days. Or rainy days. Enjoy the weather this week and give thanks.

Let go of stress

When we have a lot of stress in our lives, we can have a lot of major impacts in our lives. It can Affect our immune system and health overall. This can lead to feeling burnt out worried, tension.

Ask yourself this: "Am I really stress?"

Is what you are stressing about really worth it? Sometimes it can feel like it is very stressful, but placing top 5 stressors on paper can help assist you. See what exactly is triggering you also, is it external or is it internal? Are the expectations too unrealistic and you need to back down a little?

When we start to examine the stress, we start to realise it is not linked to anything really it is general anxiety. Take the time to reflect on yourself and say, "Is there anything I can do right now?" If you cannot do anything right now, then maybe it is not wOrth the energy placed onto this.

Here are some tips to do:

Find a quiet place and take the time out to breathe for 5 minutes with your eyes closed. Take deep inhalations right down to your belly. Do this at least 10 times to relax and take time out for a moment.

Now, take the time out to feel your body and where you might be holding onto your tension, where is it placed? Most of the common places are neck, shoulders, temple or jaw. Now visualise these areas soft and relaxed, when you relax the body relaxes. Take more deep breathes.

say to yourself "I am calm"

Now, you should be feeling a little calmer and more relaxed. Now, let's go back to the situation that was causing all this stress. Imagine you can zoom it in and out, look at it from a distance. Let's forward pace this to a time in the future. A year ahead, what would you be feeling? Now think of a friend, what would you say to a friend about this issue.

Now, it is time to journal for the next 5 mins and get those thoughts out of your head and onto paper. From this calm perspective you may get better things out of your head on how you will react to the situation.

Have fun, be yourself. Enjoy life & stay positive. - Tatiana Maslany

Daily Gratitude

DATE:

I am grateful for:

_____

_____

_____

_____

_____

_____

_____

_____

_____

_____

_____

_____

_____

_____

_____

_____

_____

_____

_____

Daily Affirmation about myself

I AM:

Happiness Scale % :

0   25   50   75   100

A friend is someone who gives you total freedom to be yourself.
Jim Morrison

Daily Gratitude

DATE:

I am grateful for:

_____

_____

_____

_____

_____

_____

_____

_____

_____

_____

_____

_____

_____

_____

_____

_____

_____

_____

Daily Affirmation about myself
I AM:

Happiness Scale % :

| 0 | 25 | 50 | 75 | 100 |

Helping one person might not change the whole world, but it could change the world for one person

Daily Gratitude

DATE:

I am grateful for:

_____

_____

_____

_____

_____

_____

_____

_____

_____

_____

_____

_____

_____

_____

_____

_____

_____

_____

_____

_____

_____

_____

Daily Affirmation about myself

I AM:

Happiness Scale % :

0   25   50   75   100

Leadership is about being authentically you and nobody else. - Alicia Wade

Daily Gratitude

DATE:

I am grateful for:

_____

_____

_____

_____

_____

_____

_____

_____

_____

_____

_____

_____

_____

_____

_____

_____

Daily Affirmation about myself
I AM:

Happiness Scale % :

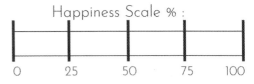

0   25   50   75   100

Life is better when you are laughing

Daily Gratitude

DATE:

I am grateful for:

_____
_____
_____
_____
_____
_____
_____
_____
_____
_____
_____
_____
_____
_____
_____
_____
_____
_____
_____

Daily Affirmation about myself
I AM:

Happiness Scale % :

0   25   50   75   100

Little by little, a little becomes a lot. - Tanzanian Proverb

Daily Gratitude

DATE:

I am grateful for:

_____

_____

_____

_____

_____

_____

_____

_____

_____

_____

_____

_____

_____

_____

_____

_____

_____

_____

Daily Affirmation about myself
I AM:

Happiness Scale % :

0   25   50   75   100

Die with memories, not dreams

Daily Gratitude

DATE:

I am grateful for:

_____

_____

_____

_____

_____

_____

_____

_____

_____

_____

_____

_____

_____

_____

_____

_____

_____

_____

_____

Daily Affirmation about myself

I AM:

Happiness Scale % :

0   25   50   75   100

Date:

Weekly Reflection
WEEK 9

Write about the 9th week of gratitude and reflect on what you noticed, felt, heard, saw and any other things you may of noticed.

_____

_____

_____

_____

_____

_____

_____

_____

_____

_____

_____

_____

_____

_____

_____

_____

_____

_____

_____

_____

_____

_____

_____

_____

_____

"When you focus on faith rather than fear, you tap into a strength to carry you over even the tallest of mountains."
Gratitude Publisher

Week 10 Challenge

PET:

Hug your pet, post a picture on Facebook or Instagram and tell everyone about them.

Respond rather than react

When something goes wrong in life, the first thing we do is react in a negative way. Reacting is a trigger of "fight or flight" instinct, it is fear based and the way we respond to situations? The way we respond, however, is a conscious choice. It is less emotional and mindful.

If you usually react to things it often helps to become more conscious of it and then see the physical signs of it, as well as, the "trigger point"

1.
Pay attention to physical signs
When you are reacting, notice what is going on in your body:
Tightness in chest
Heart racing
Muscles tensing
Feeling hot
Your breathe becoming faster

2.
Be mindful of your triggers
Tiredness
Unfairness
Feeling irritated
Ignored by others
Not listen to
Frighten
Feeling attacked by others
Annoyed by someone

3.
Make a choice
There is a list on the next page to go through how you react and what you can do to respond. Take a look and see how you can change the way you react.

You may have to fight a battle more than once to win it. - Margaret Thatcher

Daily Gratitude

DATE:

I am grateful for:

_____

_____

_____

_____

_____

_____

_____

_____

_____

_____

_____

_____

_____

_____

_____

_____

_____

_____

_____

Daily Affirmation about myself

I AM:

Happiness Scale % :

0   25   50   75   100

Believe

Daily Gratitude

DATE:

I am grateful for:

_____

_____

_____

_____

_____

_____

_____

_____

_____

_____

_____

_____

_____

_____

_____

_____

_____

_____

_____

_____

_____

Daily Affirmation about myself
I AM:

Happiness Scale % :

0   25   50   75   100

If it comes, let it. if it goes, let it.

Daily Gratitude

DATE:

I am grateful for:

_____

_____

_____

_____

_____

_____

_____

_____

_____

_____

_____

_____

_____

_____

_____

_____

_____

Daily Affirmation about myself
I AM:

Happiness Scale % :

0   25   50   75   100

I don't lose. I either win or learn...-Nelson Mandela

Daily Gratitude

DATE:

I am grateful for:

_____

_____

_____

_____

_____

_____

_____

_____

_____

_____

_____

_____

_____

_____

_____

_____

_____

_____

_____

_____

_____

Daily Affirmation about myself

I AM:

Happiness Scale % :

0   25   50   75   100

Turn your wounds into wisdom. - Oprah Winfrey

Daily Gratitude

DATE:

I am grateful for:

_____

_____

_____

_____

_____

_____

_____

_____

_____

_____

_____

_____

_____

_____

_____

_____

_____

_____

Daily Affirmation about myself
I AM:

Happiness Scale % :

0   25   50   75   100

Happiness is the highest level of success

Daily Gratitude

DATE:

I am grateful for:

_____

_____

_____

_____

_____

_____

_____

_____

_____

_____

_____

_____

_____

_____

_____

_____

_____

_____

Daily Affirmation about myself

I AM:

Happiness Scale % :

0	25	50	75	100

Fight for what you want, Don't ever give up. - Sinthuja Sinthu

Daily Gratitude

DATE:

I am grateful for:

_____

_____

_____

_____

_____

_____

_____

_____

_____

_____

_____

_____

_____

_____

_____

_____

Daily Affirmation about myself
I AM:

Happiness Scale % :

0   25   50   75   100

Weekly Reflection

WEEK 10

Write about the 10th week of gratitude and reflect on what you noticed, felt, heard, saw and any other things you may of noticed.

"If you can't change the circumstances, change the attitude. Funny thing is, when you do, you'll find that the circumstances often change."

Week 11 Challenge

FOOD:

Eat some delicious food that fuels your soul, savour it and give thanks. BE GRATEFUL! Be mindful with each bite and really take the time to enjoy each mouthful you eat this week.

What are You Avoiding?

What do I move away from or avoid in life? Why is that?

_____

_____

_____

_____

_____

What in my mind / heart / body is the worst thing(s) that could happen to me? What plans, relationships, activities have I made around these possible happenings?

_____

_____

_____

_____

_____

What past events / relationships do I want to make sure never happen again?

_____

_____

_____

_____

How will you take what you learned from this forward into your life?

_____

_____

_____

_____

_____

Life is tough, but so are you

Daily Gratitude

DATE :

I am grateful for:

_____

_____

_____

_____

_____

_____

_____

_____

_____

_____

_____

_____

_____

_____

_____

_____

_____

_____

Daily Affirmation about myself
I AM:

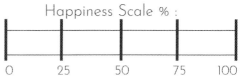

Happiness Scale % :

0   25   50   75   100

I am thankful for the people who never left

Daily Gratitude

DATE:

I am grateful for:

_____

_____

_____

_____

_____

_____

_____

_____

_____

_____

_____

_____

_____

_____

_____

_____

_____

_____

Daily Affirmation about myself
I AM:

Happiness Scale % :

0   25   50   75   100

We are creatures of habit, so make sure your habits are good ones. - Wayne Gretzky

Daily Gratitude

DATE:

I am grateful for:

_____

_____

_____

_____

_____

_____

_____

_____

_____

_____

_____

_____

_____

_____

_____

_____

_____

_____

_____

Daily Affirmation about myself

I AM:

Happiness Scale % :

| 0 | 25 | 50 | 75 | 100 |

I am calm and rested, ready for the day

Daily Gratitude

DATE:

I am grateful for:

_____

_____

_____

_____

_____

_____

_____

_____

_____

_____

_____

_____

_____

_____

_____

_____

_____

_____

_____

_____

Daily Affirmation about myself
I AM:

Happiness Scale % :

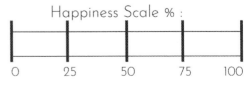

0   25   50   75   100

Today choose happiness at every chance you get

Daily Gratitude

DATE:

I am grateful for:

_____

_____

_____

_____

_____

_____

_____

_____

_____

_____

_____

_____

_____

_____

_____

_____

_____

_____

_____

_____

_____

Daily Affirmation about myself

I AM:

Happiness Scale % :

0   25   50   75   100

Today is a good day to change your life

Daily Gratitude

DATE:

I am grateful for:

_____

_____

_____

_____

_____

_____

_____

_____

_____

_____

_____

_____

_____

_____

_____

_____

_____

_____

Daily Affirmation about myself

I AM:

Happiness Scale % :

0   25   50   75   100

#gratitudeisthebestattitude

Say something kind to a stranger

Daily Gratitude

DATE:

I am grateful for:

_____

_____

_____

_____

_____

_____

_____

_____

_____

_____

_____

_____

_____

_____

_____

_____

_____

_____

_____

_____

Daily Affirmation about myself

I AM:

Happiness Scale % :

0   25   50   75   100

Date:

Weekly Reflection

WEEK 11

Write about the 11th week of gratitude and reflect on what you noticed, felt, heard, saw and any other things you may of noticed.

_____

_____

_____

_____

_____

_____

_____

_____

_____

_____

_____

_____

_____

_____

_____

_____

_____

_____

_____

_____

_____

_____

_____

"Good things come to people who wait, but better things come to those who go out and get them."
Abraham Lincoln

Week 12 Challenge

AFFIRMATIONS:

Write the words on paper or make a poster:
"I AM..." e.g. I am confident, I am worthy, I
am enough.... Place them around the house
and read them all the time for the week, see
what shifts in your mind.

Manage your energy

Your energy is so important in terms of health and wellness, start to take more notice and tune into it more mindfully. You will start to notice that different people, places and sounds all contribute to how energised you feel. It is much more than sleep, how fit we are, or what we have eaten. These are important but they are just as important as your energy too.

When we get busy, we forget about the things that energise us the most. They are the things that make us happy. They should not be second best and we should tune into doing this.

Make time for your favourite activities, feel good, feel centred, feel grounded. Then be attune to the tasks that drain your energy.

What energises you?
What drains you?
Write below:

Find a way to light a fire in your soul that compels you to act to help others

Daily Gratitude

DATE:

I am grateful for:

_____

_____

_____

_____

_____

_____

_____

_____

_____

_____

_____

_____

_____

_____

_____

_____

_____

_____

Daily Affirmation about myself

I AM:

Happiness Scale % :

0   25   50   75   100

Something amazing could happen today if you believe it.

Daily Gratitude

DATE:

I am grateful for:

_____

_____

_____

_____

_____

_____

_____

_____

_____

_____

_____

_____

_____

_____

_____

_____

_____

_____

_____

_____

_____

Daily Affirmation about myself

I AM:

Happiness Scale % :

0   25   50   75   100

Treat yourself to something you have wanted for a long time

Daily Gratitude

DATE:

I am grateful for:

_____

_____

_____

_____

_____

_____

_____

_____

_____

_____

_____

_____

_____

_____

_____

_____

_____

_____

_____

Daily Affirmation about myself
I AM:

Happiness Scale % :

0   25   50   75   100

Mindfully breathe for 5 mins.

Daily Gratitude

DATE:

I am grateful for:

_____

_____

_____

_____

_____

_____

_____

_____

_____

_____

_____

_____

_____

_____

_____

_____

_____

Daily Affirmation about myself
I AM:

Happiness Scale % :

0   25   50   75   100

Tell someone how grateful you are of them

Daily Gratitude

DATE:

I am grateful for:

_____

_____

_____

_____

_____

_____

_____

_____

_____

_____

_____

_____

_____

_____

_____

_____

_____

_____

Daily Affirmation about myself

I AM:

Happiness Scale % :

0   25   50   75   100

Say "please" and "thank you" and really mean it

Daily Gratitude

DATE:

I am grateful for:

_____

_____

_____

_____

_____

_____

_____

_____

_____

_____

_____

_____

_____

_____

_____

_____

_____

_____

Daily Affirmation about myself

I AM:

Happiness Scale % :

0   25   50   75   100

I am enough

Daily Gratitude

DATE:

I am grateful for:

_____

_____

_____

_____

_____

_____

_____

_____

_____

_____

_____

_____

_____

_____

_____

_____

_____

_____

_____

_____

Daily Affirmation about myself
I AM:

Happiness Scale % :

0   25   50   75   100

Weekly Reflection

WEEK 12

Write about the 12th week of gratitude and reflect on what you noticed, felt, heard, saw and any other things you may of noticed.

_____

_____

_____

_____

_____

_____

_____

_____

_____

_____

_____

_____

_____

_____

_____

_____

_____

_____

_____

_____

_____

"Good things come to people who wait, but better things come to those who go out and get them."

Week 13 Challenge

DRINK:

Drink at least 2L of water and notice how it fuels your body. Our bodies need it to run effectively, give it the water it needs and be conscious of this.

Intuitive Nature walking

Over the last year, i have been exploring more of more of my spirituality. I have been taught some amazing new ways by a Shamanic healer Anthea Durand and what I realised was I have been intuitive walking in nature for quite some time. Now, with both our powers we can assist you with your overall energy and drive. I love to go into nature and go for walks to allow creative flow to come through and for me to just BE and for my mind to WANDER. All you need to do is find a large area of nature, or beach, or forest, or bush land. Allow yourself to be moved by nature.

Whenever you feel drawn to a tree or a rock or a piece of land go to it. Get really immersed into nature notice what you see, hear, feel and notice all around you. Be laying down, sit up, close your eyes. Follow what your mind tells you to do.
It's time to switch off and BE with on in nature.
Notice all the beautiful things all around you.
Trust the whole walk and process.
Trust your intuition to guide you all around nature.

Walk for at least 20mins, go for longer. I sometimes get caught up for 6-8 hours at a time. Let yourself be free and carefree. Take journal and write down anything that comes to your mind. I have written my best work in nature.

It is amazing how you feel after this experience.

Find time to enjoy the sunshine today

Daily Gratitude

DATE:

I am grateful for:

_____

_____

_____

_____

_____

_____

_____

_____

_____

_____

_____

_____

_____

_____

_____

_____

_____

_____

_____

Daily Affirmation about myself

I AM:

Happiness Scale % :

0   25   50   75   100

We are all made of the stars, so remember to shine

Daily Gratitude

DATE:

I am grateful for:

_____

_____

_____

_____

_____

_____

_____

_____

_____

_____

_____

_____

_____

_____

_____

_____

Daily Affirmation about myself

I AM:

Happiness Scale % :

0   25   50   75   100

Go somewhere you have never been before

Daily Gratitude

DATE:

I am grateful for:

_____

_____

_____

_____

_____

_____

_____

_____

_____

_____

_____

_____

_____

_____

_____

_____

_____

_____

_____

Daily Affirmation about myself
I AM:

Happiness Scale % :

0   25   50   75   100

Daily Gratitude

DATE:

I am grateful for:

_____

_____

_____

_____

_____

_____

_____

_____

_____

_____

_____

_____

_____

_____

_____

_____

_____

_____

_____

_____

_____

Daily Affirmation about myself

I AM:

Happiness Scale % :

0   25   50   75   100

You can bear almost anything if you have a reason to

Daily Gratitude

DATE:

I am grateful for:

_____

_____

_____

_____

_____

_____

_____

_____

_____

_____

_____

_____

_____

_____

_____

_____

_____

_____

_____

_____

_____

_____

Daily Affirmation about myself

I AM:

Happiness Scale % :

0   25   50   75   100

Think to achieve, Think BIG. - Alicia Wade

Daily Gratitude

DATE:

I am grateful for:

_____

_____

_____

_____

_____

_____

_____

_____

_____

_____

_____

_____

_____

_____

_____

_____

_____

_____

_____

Daily Affirmation about myself

I AM:

Happiness Scale % :

0   25   50   75   100

Donate your time to someone or something

Daily Gratitude

DATE:

I am grateful for:

_____

_____

_____

_____

_____

_____

_____

_____

_____

_____

_____

_____

_____

_____

_____

_____

_____

_____

_____

_____

Daily Affirmation about myself
I AM:

Happiness Scale % :

0   25   50   75   100

Date:

Weekly Reflection
WEEK13

Write about the 13th week of gratitude and reflect on what you noticed, felt, heard, saw and any other things you may of noticed.

"Pain makes you stronger, fear makes you braver, heartbreak makes you wiser."
Drake

Week 14 Challenge

MUSIC:

Put on your favourite music. Dance, sing and be merry. Appreciate the music you hear! HAVE FUN THIS WEEK!

Whispers in your mind

Take the time out to go out of contact for a moment in time, for a walk on the beach, for a stroll in nature. Whatever to take the time out and BE. Start to listen to the thoughts that come to your mind and write down anything that comes up for you in this present time. They may come to you slowly, they may be quick and fast and flood through your mind. Whatever comes just write it down and get it out of your mind and be in tune with your mind, body and soul.

Breathe deeply and allow yourself to be fully present to YOU.

You may have a feeling come through, write this down. Whatever comes through to you, just write it down and listen to the whispers in your mind.

Feel the emotions and treasure the beauty all around you. It is now time to appreciate every detail around you.

The more you focus on the good things, the better your life will become

Daily Gratitude

DATE:

I am grateful for:

_____

_____

_____

_____

_____

_____

_____

_____

_____

_____

_____

_____

_____

_____

_____

_____

_____

Daily Affirmation about myself
I AM:

Happiness Scale % :

0   25   50   75   100

It really is the simple things in life that matter

Daily Gratitude

DATE:

I am grateful for:

_____

_____

_____

_____

_____

_____

_____

_____

_____

_____

_____

_____

_____

_____

_____

_____

_____

_____

_____

_____

Daily Affirmation about myself

I AM:

Happiness Scale % :

0   25   50   75   100

If you want it, go get it...- Chris Gardener

Daily Gratitude

DATE:

I am grateful for:

_____

_____

_____

_____

_____

_____

_____

_____

_____

_____

_____

_____

_____

_____

_____

_____

_____

Daily Affirmation about myself
I AM:

Happiness Scale % :

0   25   50   75   100

Follow your heart but take your brain with you. - Alfred Adler

Daily Gratitude

DATE:

I am grateful for:

_____

_____

_____

_____

_____

_____

_____

_____

_____

_____

_____

_____

_____

_____

_____

_____

_____

_____

Daily Affirmation about myself
I AM:

Happiness Scale % :

0   25   50   75   100

Never judge a book by it's cover

Daily Gratitude

DATE:

I am grateful for:

_____

_____

_____

_____

_____

_____

_____

_____

_____

_____

_____

_____

_____

_____

_____

_____

_____

_____

_____

_____

Daily Affirmation about myself

I AM:

Happiness Scale % :

0   25   50   75   100

You may see me struggle, but you will never see me quit

Daily Gratitude

DATE:

I am grateful for:

_____

_____

_____

_____

_____

_____

_____

_____

_____

_____

_____

_____

_____

_____

_____

_____

_____

_____

Daily Affirmation about myself
I AM:

Happiness Scale % :

0   25   50   75   100

It costs you $0 to believe in yourself

Daily Gratitude

DATE:

I am grateful for:

_____

_____

_____

_____

_____

_____

_____

_____

_____

_____

_____

_____

_____

_____

_____

_____

_____

Daily Affirmation about myself
I AM:

Happiness Scale % :

0   25   50   75   100

Date:

Weekly Reflection
WEEK 14

Write about the 14th week of gratitude and reflect on what you noticed, felt, heard, saw and any other things you may of noticed.

_____

_____

_____

_____

_____

_____

_____

_____

_____

_____

_____

_____

_____

_____

_____

_____

_____

_____

_____

_____

_____

_____

_____

_____

Happiness Scale % :

0   25   50   75   100

"Never apologize for having high standards, people who really want to be in your life will rise and meet them."

Ziad K. Abdelnour

Week 15

Challenge

LISTEN:

Take the time today to really listen to all sounds around you. Be really present in the moment to notice and hear things.

Write a letter to self

Write a letter to yourself: What does your ideal life look like? what does it sound like? What do you want to be remembered by? What is your true souls purpose? Start writing and let the visuals, thoughts flow now...

_____

_____

_____

_____

_____

_____

_____

_____

_____

_____

_____

_____

_____

_____

_____

_____

_____

_____

_____

_____

_____

_____

_____

Stop doubting yourself, work hard, and make it happen

Daily Gratitude

DATE:

I am grateful for:

_____

_____

_____

_____

_____

_____

_____

_____

_____

_____

_____

_____

_____

_____

_____

_____

_____

_____

_____

Daily Affirmation about myself
I AM:

Happiness Scale % :

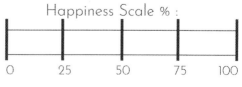

0   25   50   75   100

Remember to be kind to yourself

Daily Gratitude

DATE:

I am grateful for:

_____

_____

_____

_____

_____

_____

_____

_____

_____

_____

_____

_____

_____

_____

_____

_____

_____

_____

Daily Affirmation about myself

I AM:

Happiness Scale % :

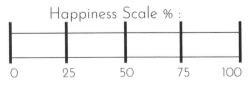

0   25   50   75   100

Heal yourself first, the rest will come later.

Daily Gratitude

DATE :

I am grateful for:

_____

_____

_____

_____

_____

_____

_____

_____

_____

_____

_____

_____

_____

_____

_____

_____

_____

_____

_____

Daily Affirmation about myself

I AM:

Happiness Scale % :

0   25   50   75   100

Your current location is not your final destination

Daily Gratitude

DATE:

I am grateful for:

_____

_____

_____

_____

_____

_____

_____

_____

_____

_____

_____

_____

_____

_____

_____

_____

_____

_____

Daily Affirmation about myself
I AM:

Happiness Scale % :

0   25   50   75   100

Before you give up, think of why you held on for so long

Daily Gratitude

DATE:

I am grateful for:

_____

_____

_____

_____

_____

_____

_____

_____

_____

_____

_____

_____

_____

_____

_____

_____

_____

_____

Daily Affirmation about myself

I AM:

Happiness Scale % :

0   25   50   75   100

Don't give up on the person you are becoming

Daily Gratitude

DATE:

I am grateful for:

_____

_____

_____

_____

_____

_____

_____

_____

_____

_____

_____

_____

_____

_____

_____

_____

_____

_____

_____

_____

_____

Daily Affirmation about myself

I AM:

Happiness Scale % :

0   25   50   75   100

The secret is that you must believe in what you can't yet see. -
Gaurang Sharma GS

Daily Gratitude

DATE:

I am grateful for:

_____

_____

_____

_____

_____

_____

_____

_____

_____

_____

_____

_____

_____

_____

_____

_____

_____

Daily Affirmation about myself
I AM:

Happiness Scale % :

0   25   50   75   100

Weekly Reflection

WEEK 16

Write about the 16th week of gratitude and reflect on what you noticed, felt, heard, saw and any other things you may of noticed.

"If you can't stop thinking about it, it's probably something worth going after."

Week 16 Challenge

BED:

Go to bed a little earlier and be grateful for 3 things before sleeping.

Thank you Mother

We all have a mother,
we all know that our mothers tried their best to do what was right for them and us.
We cannot blame them for the things that have happened, only reflect on the life's teaching that have been taught to us to either follow or change the way we BE, DO, GIVE AND HAVE...

What sacrifices did your mother make for you?

_____

_____

_____

What are you most grateful for about your mother?

_____

_____

_____

What lessons did she teach you?

_____

_____

_____

What did you yearn for as you got older that your mother was not able to give you?

_____

_____

_____

How can you give this to yourself?

_____

_____

_____

Sometimes, your only available form of transportation is a leap in faith. - Margaret Shepard

Daily Gratitude

DATE:

I am grateful for:

_____

_____

_____

_____

_____

_____

_____

_____

_____

_____

_____

_____

_____

_____

_____

_____

_____

_____

_____

Daily Affirmation about myself
I AM:

Happiness Scale % :

0   25   50   75   100

Never stop being yourself in order to please others

Daily Gratitude

DATE:

I am grateful for:

_____

_____

_____

_____

_____

_____

_____

_____

_____

_____

_____

_____

_____

_____

_____

_____

_____

Daily Affirmation about myself
I AM:

Happiness Scale % :

0   25   50   75   100

Daily Gratitude

DATE:

I am grateful for:

_____

_____

_____

_____

_____

_____

_____

_____

_____

_____

_____

_____

_____

_____

_____

_____

_____

_____

_____

Daily Affirmation about myself
I AM:

Happiness Scale % :

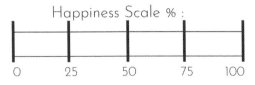

0   25   50   75   100

Get comfortable with being alone, it will empower you. - Jonathan Tropper

Daily Gratitude

DATE:

I am grateful for:

_____

_____

_____

_____

_____

_____

_____

_____

_____

_____

_____

_____

_____

_____

_____

_____

_____

_____

_____

_____

_____

_____

Daily Affirmation about myself

I AM:

Happiness Scale % :

0   25   50   75   100

If you are tired learn to rest, not quit

Daily Gratitude

D A T E :

I am grateful for:

_____

_____

_____

_____

_____

_____

_____

_____

_____

_____

_____

_____

_____

_____

_____

_____

_____

Daily Affirmation about myself
I AM:

Happiness Scale % :

0   25   50   75   100

Here is the sign you've been waiting for: Don't quit

Daily Gratitude

DATE:

I am grateful for:

_____

_____

_____

_____

_____

_____

_____

_____

_____

_____

_____

_____

_____

_____

_____

_____

Daily Affirmation about myself
I AM:

Happiness Scale % :

0   25   50   75   100

Strength also looks like taking a break to nurture, nourish, restore and align yourself. - Lalah Delia

Daily Gratitude

DATE:

I am grateful for:

_____

_____

_____

_____

_____

_____

_____

_____

_____

_____

_____

_____

_____

_____

_____

_____

_____

_____

Daily Affirmation about myself
I AM:

Happiness Scale % :

0   25   50   75   100

Date:

Weekly Reflection
WEEK 16

Write about the 16th week of gratitude and reflect on what you noticed, felt, heard, saw and any other things you may of noticed.

"Love yourself enough to never lower your standards for anyone."

#gratitudeisthebestattitude

Week 17

Challenge

FUN:

Do something you love and find fun to do!

Show up!

Where in your life are you hiding?

_____

_____

_____

_____

_____

_____

What would happen if you allowed yourself to be seen fully and heard fully?

_____

_____

_____

_____

_____

_____

_____

_____

_____

_____

_____

_____

_____

_____

_____

_____

_____

_____

_____

_____

It is so empowering to say, "this is no longer serving me"
and walking away

Daily Gratitude

DATE:

I am grateful for:

_____

_____

_____

_____

_____

_____

_____

_____

_____

_____

_____

_____

_____

_____

_____

_____

_____

_____

Daily Affirmation about myself
I AM:

Happiness Scale % :

0   25   50   75   100

Blessed, thankful and focused

Daily Gratitude

DATE:

I am grateful for:

_____

_____

_____

_____

_____

_____

_____

_____

_____

_____

_____

_____

_____

_____

_____

_____

_____

_____

_____

_____

Daily Affirmation about myself

I AM:

Happiness Scale % :

0   25   50   75   100

Don't just be good to others. Be good to yourself as well.

Daily Gratitude

DATE :

I am grateful for:

_____

_____

_____

_____

_____

_____

_____

_____

_____

_____

_____

_____

_____

_____

_____

_____

_____

_____

Daily Affirmation about myself
I AM:

Happiness Scale % :

0   25   50   75   100

Make your vision so clear that your fears become irrelevant

Daily Gratitude

DATE:

I am grateful for:

_____

_____

_____

_____

_____

_____

_____

_____

_____

_____

_____

_____

_____

_____

_____

_____

_____

_____

Daily Affirmation about myself

I AM:

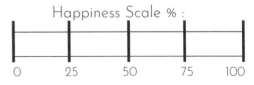

Happiness Scale % :

0   25   50   75   100

A positive mindset provides positive results

Daily Gratitude

DATE:

I am grateful for:

_____
_____
_____
_____
_____
_____
_____
_____
_____
_____
_____
_____
_____
_____
_____
_____
_____
_____
_____
_____

Daily Affirmation about myself

I AM:

Happiness Scale % :

0   25   50   75   100

You are enough

Daily Gratitude

DATE:

I am grateful for:

_____

_____

_____

_____

_____

_____

_____

_____

_____

_____

_____

_____

_____

_____

_____

_____

_____

Daily Affirmation about myself
I AM:

Happiness Scale % :

0   25   50   75   100

Someone who cares about you will never gain power from making you weak

Daily Gratitude

DATE:

I am grateful for:

_____
_____
_____
_____
_____
_____
_____
_____
_____
_____
_____
_____
_____
_____
_____
_____
_____

Daily Affirmation about myself

I AM:

Happiness Scale % :

0   25   50   75   100

Date:

Weekly Reflection

WEEK 17

Write about the 17th week of gratitude and reflect on what you noticed, felt, heard, saw and any other things you may of noticed.

"Don't talk, just act. Don't say, just show. Don't promise, just prove."

Week 18 Challenge

LAUGH:

Watch a funny movie and have a good laugh today!

#gratitudeisthebestattitude

Life's Reflection

Get an A4 piece of paper, draw a line horizontally from left to right. This will be your timeline. From the far left is from the time you were born and the far right is where you are in the present moment in time.

Start adding dots in this timeline to identify all the significant moments in your life, happy days with family or friends, sad moments when family members have passed, or moments that really stand out for you.

At each moment, reflect and think then write: what did you need to hear at that moment? write it down.

Take the time to really delve deep and look at each moment in time. Once this is completed, look back over your notes and see if there is a common thread of moments in time.

When you stop chasing the wrong things, you give the right things a chance to catch up to you

Daily Gratitude

DATE:

I am grateful for:

_____

_____

_____

_____

_____

_____

_____

_____

_____

_____

_____

_____

_____

_____

_____

_____

_____

_____

Daily Affirmation about myself
I AM:

Happiness Scale % :

0   25   50   75   100

Don't commit to the sprint, commit to the marathon. - Yulin Lee

Daily Gratitude

DATE:

I am grateful for:

_____

_____

_____

_____

_____

_____

_____

_____

_____

_____

_____

_____

_____

_____

_____

_____

_____

_____

_____

_____

Daily Affirmation about myself

I AM:

Happiness Scale % :

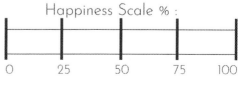

0   25   50   75   100

Design your life around moments not things

Daily Gratitude

DATE:

I am grateful for:

_____

_____

_____

_____

_____

_____

_____

_____

_____

_____

_____

_____

_____

_____

_____

_____

_____

_____

Daily Affirmation about myself
I AM:

Happiness Scale % :

0   25   50   75   100

Love your life and it will love you back

Daily Gratitude

DATE:

I am grateful for:

_____

_____

_____

_____

_____

_____

_____

_____

_____

_____

_____

_____

_____

_____

_____

_____

_____

_____

_____

_____

Daily Affirmation about myself
I AM:

Happiness Scale % :

0   25   50   75   100

Daily Gratitude

DATE:

I am grateful for:

_____

_____

_____

_____

_____

_____

_____

_____

_____

_____

_____

_____

_____

_____

_____

_____

_____

_____

Daily Affirmation about myself
I AM:

Happiness Scale % :

0   25   50   75   100

If you don't go after what you want, you'll never get it. - Nora Roberts

Daily Gratitude

DATE:

I am grateful for:

_____

_____

_____

_____

_____

_____

_____

_____

_____

_____

_____

_____

_____

_____

_____

_____

_____

_____

_____

Daily Affirmation about myself

I AM:

Happiness Scale % :

0   25   50   75   100

Be such a good soul that people crave your vibe

Daily Gratitude

DATE:

I am grateful for:

_____

_____

_____

_____

_____

_____

_____

_____

_____

_____

_____

_____

_____

_____

_____

_____

_____

Daily Affirmation about myself
I AM:

Happiness Scale % :

0   25   50   75   100

Date:

Weekly Reflection
WEEK 18

Write about the 18th week of gratitude and reflect on what you noticed, felt, heard, saw and any other things you may of noticed.

_____

_____

_____

_____

_____

_____

_____

_____

_____

_____

_____

_____

_____

_____

_____

_____

_____

_____

_____

_____

_____

_____

_____

"As you close your eyes tonight, may you know how blessed you are and celebrate with gratitude."

Week 19 Challenge

MINDFULNESS:

Time to do a mindful activity like colouring in.
Let your mind wander and not have to think
all week either in the morning or the evening
for a couple of hours and let your mind relax.

Meditation on light

- Find a comfortable seated position and shift your weight to find a place of balance with the spine straight and shoulders relaxed. (You can lie down if sitting is not comfortable for you).

- Feel into your breathe in and out.

- Notice what it feels like in your body.

- As you take the breathes, take the time to relax, imagine a point of light on the top of your head.

- Take the time to focus your attention on the light as you breathe.

- Notice the quality of light, its vibration, its flavour.

- Keep breathing and observing the light.

- If your mind wanders to thinking, gentle guide it back to observing and feeling into the breathe and seeing the light.

- After this is completed, stretch, drink some water, journal your thoughts.

PLEASE NOTE:

You can have the light focus point of the light at your heart centre or in the centre of your head. When you have it in different locations there will be different feelings and emotions, as well as, visuals.

Sometimes you have to disconnect from everything externally and spend time with yourself

Daily Gratitude

DATE:

I am grateful for:

_____

_____

_____

_____

_____

_____

_____

_____

_____

_____

_____

_____

_____

_____

_____

_____

_____

_____

Daily Affirmation about myself

I AM:

Happiness Scale % :

0   25   50   75   100

Surround yourself with only those who will force you to level up

Daily Gratitude

DATE:

I am grateful for:

_____

_____

_____

_____

_____

_____

_____

_____

_____

_____

_____

_____

_____

_____

_____

_____

_____

_____

Daily Affirmation about myself
I AM:

Happiness Scale % :

0   25   50   75   100

Some days there won't be a song in your heart, sing anyway. -
Emory Austin

Daily Gratitude

DATE:

I am grateful for:

_____
_____
_____
_____
_____
_____
_____
_____
_____
_____
_____
_____
_____
_____
_____
_____
_____

Daily Affirmation about myself
I AM:

Happiness Scale % :

0   25   50   75   100

You are unique

Daily Gratitude

DATE:

I am grateful for:

_____

_____

_____

_____

_____

_____

_____

_____

_____

_____

_____

_____

_____

_____

_____

_____

_____

_____

Daily Affirmation about myself
I AM:

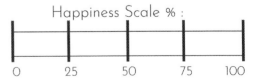

Happiness Scale % :

0   25   50   75   100

The secret to living is giving. - Tony Robbins

Daily Gratitude

DATE:

I am grateful for:

_____

_____

_____

_____

_____

_____

_____

_____

_____

_____

_____

_____

_____

_____

_____

_____

Daily Affirmation about myself

I AM:

Happiness Scale % :

0   25   50   75   100

Desire is the first element of realisation. - Tony Robbins

Daily Gratitude

DATE:

I am grateful for:

_____

_____

_____

_____

_____

_____

_____

_____

_____

_____

_____

_____

_____

_____

_____

_____

_____

_____

_____

_____

_____

Daily Affirmation about myself

I AM:

Happiness Scale % :

0   25   50   75   100

When you are grateful fear disappears and abundance appears. - Tony Robbins

Daily Gratitude

DATE :

I am grateful for:

_____

_____

_____

_____

_____

_____

_____

_____

_____

_____

_____

_____

_____

_____

_____

_____

_____

_____

Daily Affirmation about myself

I AM:

Happiness Scale % :

0   25   50   75   100

Weekly Reflection

WEEK 19

Write about the 19th week of gratitude and reflect on what you noticed, felt, heard, saw and any other things you may of noticed.

_____

_____

_____

_____

_____

_____

_____

_____

_____

_____

_____

_____

_____

_____

_____

_____

_____

_____

_____

_____

_____

_____

_____

_____

_____

"Happiness depends on ourselves."

Aristotle

Week 20 Challenge

BOOK:

Take the time out to slow down and read a book today.

Meditation on loving kindness

1. Find a comfortable seated position and shift your weight to find a place of balance with the spine straight and shoulders relaxed. (You can lie down if sitting is not comfortable for you).
2. Feel into your breathe in and out.
3. Notice what it feels like in your body.
4. Soften your face, your jaw, your eyes, and even the the feeling of a gentle smile on the inside.
5. As you take your next breathe in, feel into the love in your heart, perhaps recall the times you have felt love and kindness.
6. Breathe in deeply - feel the love within you, feel your capacity for love.
7. Feel the energy of your heart growing stronger as you focus now on love.
8. Allow yourself to feel the love for yourself.
9. Take the time to breathe and the feelings of kindness.
10. On the inhale, say quietly or silently, "I am loved."
11. On the exhale say to yourself silently, "I am love"
12. Keep breathing slowly and keep feeling the feelings.
13. If your mind wanders to thinking, gentle guide it back to observing and feeling into the breathe and repeat the words in your mind, "I am loved." and "I am love"

Determination is the wake up call to the human will. - Tony Robbins

Daily Gratitude

DATE:

I am grateful for:

_____

_____

_____

_____

_____

_____

_____

_____

_____

_____

_____

_____

_____

_____

_____

_____

_____

Daily Affirmation about myself
I AM:

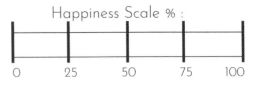

Happiness Scale % :

0   25   50   75   100

Every problem is a gift - without problems we would not grow. -
Tony Robbins

Daily Gratitude

DATE:

I am grateful for:

_____

_____

_____

_____

_____

_____

_____

_____

_____

_____

_____

_____

_____

_____

_____

_____

_____

_____

_____

Daily Affirmation about myself
I AM:

Happiness Scale % :

0   25   50   75   100

One day or day one, You decide...

Daily Gratitude

DATE:

I am grateful for:

_____
_____
_____
_____
_____
_____
_____
_____
_____
_____
_____
_____
_____
_____
_____
_____
_____
_____

Daily Affirmation about myself
I AM:

Happiness Scale % :

0   25   50   75   100

Keep it real or keep it moving...

Daily Gratitude

DATE:

I am grateful for:

_____

_____

_____

_____

_____

_____

_____

_____

_____

_____

_____

_____

_____

_____

_____

_____

_____

_____

_____

_____

_____

Daily Affirmation about myself

I AM:

Happiness Scale % :

0   25   50   75   100

You will never change your life until you change something you do.
- John C. Maxwell

Daily Gratitude

DATE:

I am grateful for:

_____

_____

_____

_____

_____

_____

_____

_____

_____

_____

_____

_____

_____

_____

_____

_____

_____

_____

Daily Affirmation about myself
I AM:

Happiness Scale % :

0   25   50   75   100

There are two types of pains, one that hurts you and the other that changes you

Daily Gratitude

DATE :

I am grateful for:

_____

_____

_____

_____

_____

_____

_____

_____

_____

_____

_____

_____

_____

_____

_____

_____

_____

_____

Daily Affirmation about myself

I AM:

Happiness Scale % :

0   25   50   75   100

Your setback is the platform for your comeback

Daily Gratitude

DATE:

I am grateful for:

_____

_____

_____

_____

_____

_____

_____

_____

_____

_____

_____

_____

_____

_____

_____

_____

_____

_____

_____

Daily Affirmation about myself

I AM:

Happiness Scale % :

0   25   50   75   100

Weekly Reflection

WEEK 20

Write about the 20th week of gratitude and reflect on what you noticed, felt, heard, saw and any other things you may of noticed.

_____

_____

_____

_____

_____

_____

_____

_____

_____

_____

_____

_____

_____

_____

_____

_____

_____

_____

_____

_____

_____

_____

_____

_____

_____

_____

_____

_____

"Stop looking for happiness in the same place you lost it."

Week 21 Challenge

BODY:

Time to look in the mirror and appreciate YOU, ALL of you!

Slow down... RELAX...

Time to take a little bit of time to slow down and relax a little bit more in your world. Are you rushing and going out of control and need to STOP!
How are you running throughout the day?
Take the time to check in on yourself throughout the day and see where you are travelling.

Some ideas to slow it down and remind yourself:

- Conversations with people can go at a slower pace.
- Walk slower.
- Chew for longer periods of time and slow it down with chewing.
- Get to you appointments earlier - see how you can get there earlier.
- When writing emails - slow it down, save it as a draft and then re-read it before sending.
- Instead of saying "yes" to people, tell someone you can get back to them about a time and a place to meet or what you need to organise in your life. When you come back you will feel more at ease with organising a time to meet.
- Drink more slowly, enjoy the taste of the drink you are drinking: tea, water, fruit water.
- Take the time to do one thing at a time instead of many things.

True leaders don't create followers. They create more leaders. -
Tom Peters

Daily Gratitude

DATE:

I am grateful for:

_____

_____

_____

_____

_____

_____

_____

_____

_____

_____

_____

_____

_____

_____

_____

_____

_____

_____

Daily Affirmation about myself
I AM:

Happiness Scale % :

0   25   50   75   100

Just play, have fun, enjoy the game. - Michael Jordan

Daily Gratitude

DATE:

I am grateful for:

_____

_____

_____

_____

_____

_____

_____

_____

_____

_____

_____

_____

_____

_____

_____

_____

_____

_____

Daily Affirmation about myself
I AM:

Happiness Scale % :

0   25   50   75   100

Be kind. Be Caring.

Daily Gratitude

DATE:

I am grateful for:

_____
_____
_____
_____
_____
_____
_____
_____
_____
_____
_____
_____
_____
_____
_____
_____
_____
_____

Daily Affirmation about myself
I AM:

Happiness Scale % :

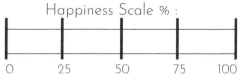

0   25   50   75   100

A friend is someone who gives you total freedom to be yourself.
Jim Morrison

Daily Gratitude

DATE:

I am grateful for:

_____

_____

_____

_____

_____

_____

_____

_____

_____

_____

_____

_____

_____

_____

_____

_____

_____

_____

_____

Daily Affirmation about myself
I AM:

Happiness Scale % :

0   25   50   75   100

Helping one person might not change the whole world, but it could change the world for one person

Daily Gratitude

DATE:

I am grateful for:

_____

_____

_____

_____

_____

_____

_____

_____

_____

_____

_____

_____

_____

_____

_____

_____

_____

_____

Daily Affirmation about myself

I AM:

Happiness Scale % :

0   25   50   75   100

Give a compliment to someone today.

Daily Gratitude

DATE:

I am grateful for:

_____

_____

_____

_____

_____

_____

_____

_____

_____

_____

_____

_____

_____

_____

_____

_____

_____

_____

_____

Daily Affirmation about myself

I AM:

Happiness Scale % :

0   25   50   75   100

Success is doing what you want to do, when you want, where you want, with whom you want as much as you want. - Tony Robbins

Daily Gratitude

DATE:

I am grateful for:

_____

_____

_____

_____

_____

_____

_____

_____

_____

_____

_____

_____

_____

_____

_____

_____

_____

Daily Affirmation about myself
I AM:

Happiness Scale % :

0   25   50   75   100

Date:

Weekly Reflection

WEEK 21

Write about the 21st week of gratitude and reflect on what you noticed, felt, heard, saw and any other things you may of noticed.

_____

_____

_____

_____

_____

_____

_____

_____

_____

_____

_____

_____

_____

_____

_____

_____

_____

_____

_____

_____

_____

_____

_____

_____

_____

"When writing the story of your life, don't let anyone else hold the pen."

Harley Davidson

Week 22

Challenge

PEOPLE:

Send a message to someone who has helped in the last month and thank them.

Bring in the good

Our minds are very powerful in regards to what it thinks and feels and the way it runs our body automatically. It also tends to naturally be drawn to the negative mindset. Which can bring us down and feel horrible from time to time.

Rick Hanson is a neuropsychologist has suggested we can balance this out with positive vibes and "take in the good".

What we need to do as a human race is really notice the positive things that happen in our life to cultivate the good. Really enjoy them, really feel them, really acknowledge them, actively seek them out all the time.

If we do this for long enough we can change the pathways in our mind and make it easier for us to feel more positive.

It works!

In your phone, add in a reminder throughout the day reminding and alerting you to check in and then reflect on what has been positive throughout the day. You morning coffee, a chat with a friend, completing a task or project you have been working on.

For 30 seconds, you need to cultivate positive thoughts in your mind. Experience all the sensations in your body and embody what you feel, hear and think. Holding this positive thought can create change in the mind.

Visualise good things- this can change the images within the mind too.

Happiness is enjoying the little things in life

Daily Gratitude

DATE:

I am grateful for:

_____

_____

_____

_____

_____

_____

_____

_____

_____

_____

_____

_____

_____

_____

_____

_____

_____

Daily Affirmation about myself
I AM:

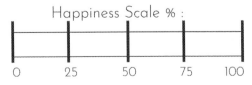

Happiness Scale % :

0   25   50   75   100

Failure isn't the opposite of success, it's part of success. - Arianna Huffington

Daily Gratitude

DATE:

I am grateful for:

_____

_____

_____

_____

_____

_____

_____

_____

_____

_____

_____

_____

_____

_____

_____

_____

_____

_____

Daily Affirmation about myself

I AM:

Happiness Scale % :

0   25   50   75   100

Do more things that make you forget your phone

Daily Gratitude

DATE:

I am grateful for:

_____

_____

_____

_____

_____

_____

_____

_____

_____

_____

_____

_____

_____

_____

_____

_____

_____

Daily Affirmation about myself
I AM:

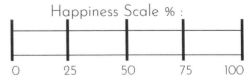

Happiness Scale % :

0   25   50   75   100

Climb the mountain so you can see the world, not so the world can see you. - David Mccullough

Daily Gratitude

DATE:

I am grateful for:

_____

_____

_____

_____

_____

_____

_____

_____

_____

_____

_____

_____

_____

_____

_____

_____

_____

_____

Daily Affirmation about myself

I AM:

Happiness Scale % :

0   25   50   75   100

One day you'll laugh at how much you let this matter. - Morley

Daily Gratitude

DATE:

I am grateful for:

_____

_____

_____

_____

_____

_____

_____

_____

_____

_____

_____

_____

_____

_____

_____

_____

_____

_____

_____

_____

Daily Affirmation about myself
I AM:

Happiness Scale % :

0   25   50   75   100

Chase your dreams not people

Daily Gratitude

DATE:

I am grateful for:

_____

_____

_____

_____

_____

_____

_____

_____

_____

_____

_____

_____

_____

_____

_____

_____

_____

_____

Daily Affirmation about myself
I AM:

Happiness Scale % :

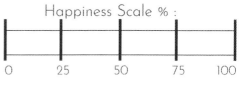

0   25   50   75   100

I hope you always find a reason to smile

Daily Gratitude

DATE:

I am grateful for:

_____

_____

_____

_____

_____

_____

_____

_____

_____

_____

_____

_____

_____

_____

_____

_____

_____

_____

_____

Daily Affirmation about myself
I AM:

Happiness Scale % :

0   25   50   75   100

Weekly Reflection

WEEK 22

Write about the 22nd week of gratitude and reflect on what you noticed, felt, heard, saw and any other things you may of noticed.

"Life's challenges are not supposed to paralyze you, they're supposed to help you discover who you are."
Bernice Johnson Reagon

Week 23

Challenge

HOME:

Get cozy on the lounge and enjoy a good cup of tea of cacao.

What makes you happy?

Now is the time to think about all the things that bring in happiness to your life - big, small and all in between. Whatever gives you that smile on your dial, whatever gives you energy, whatever gives you drive or excitement. Whatever gives you passion or meaning. Start a list here and write them all down:

You have two choices: 1. Do it now 2. Regret it later. - Kiran Mistry

Daily Gratitude

DATE:

I am grateful for:

_____

_____

_____

_____

_____

_____

_____

_____

_____

_____

_____

_____

_____

_____

_____

_____

_____

_____

_____

_____

_____

Daily Affirmation about myself
I AM:

Happiness Scale % :

0   25   50   75   100

Don't give up. Your day will come. It's just a matter of time

Daily Gratitude

DATE:

I am grateful for:

_____

_____

_____

_____

_____

_____

_____

_____

_____

_____

_____

_____

_____

_____

_____

_____

_____

_____

Daily Affirmation about myself
I AM:

Happiness Scale % :

0   25   50   75   100

Daily Gratitude

DATE :

I am grateful for:

_____

_____

_____

_____

_____

_____

_____

_____

_____

_____

_____

_____

_____

_____

_____

_____

_____

_____

Daily Affirmation about myself

I AM:

Happiness Scale % :

0   25   50   75   100

Mention someone who made your year better

Daily Gratitude

DATE:

I am grateful for:

_____
_____
_____
_____
_____
_____
_____
_____
_____
_____
_____
_____
_____
_____
_____
_____
_____
_____

Daily Affirmation about myself
I AM:

Happiness Scale % :

0   25   50   75   100

Do what makes you happy because you'll be criticized anyway

Daily Gratitude

DATE :

I am grateful for:

_____
_____
_____
_____
_____
_____
_____
_____
_____
_____
_____
_____
_____
_____
_____
_____
_____
_____
_____
_____

Daily Affirmation about myself
I AM:

Happiness Scale % :

0   25   50   75   100

Let things come and go. The things that are meant to stay will stay

Daily Gratitude

DATE:

I am grateful for:

_____

_____

_____

_____

_____

_____

_____

_____

_____

_____

_____

_____

_____

_____

_____

_____

_____

_____

_____

Daily Affirmation about myself
I AM:

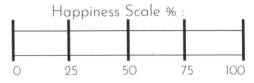

Happiness Scale % :

0   25   50   75   100

Good times are coming. Have patience

Daily Gratitude

DATE:

I am grateful for:

_____

_____

_____

_____

_____

_____

_____

_____

_____

_____

_____

_____

_____

_____

_____

_____

_____

_____

Daily Affirmation about myself
I AM:

Happiness Scale % :

0   25   50   75   100

Date:

Weekly Reflection

WEEK 23

Write about the 23rd week of gratitude and reflect on what you noticed, felt, heard, saw and any other things you may of noticed.

_____

_____

_____

_____

_____

_____

_____

_____

_____

_____

_____

_____

_____

_____

_____

_____

_____

_____

_____

_____

_____

_____

_____

"Work while they sleep.
Learn while they party.
Save while they spend.
Live like they dream."

Week 24

Challenge

BATH:

Allow yourself to soak in the bath for 30 mins and RELAX!

Reverse bucket list

We all have a bucket list of things we have done, now it is time to reverse engineer this and think of all the things you have done. Bucket lists are the things you want to do before you pass on. This one is all about celebrating what you have done. Where have you been? What have you done? What have you achieved? What experiences have you had? Take the time to inspire yourself on all the things you have done. This is a great reminder to bring back happiness and joy to your life!

Don't cry because it's over smile because it happened. - Dr Seuss

Daily Gratitude

DATE:

I am grateful for:

_____

_____

_____

_____

_____

_____

_____

_____

_____

_____

_____

_____

_____

_____

_____

_____

_____

_____

Daily Affirmation about myself
I AM:

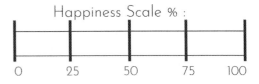

Happiness Scale % :

0   25   50   75   100

A year from now you will wish you had started today. - Karen Lamb

Daily Gratitude

DATE:

I am grateful for:

_____

_____

_____

_____

_____

_____

_____

_____

_____

_____

_____

_____

_____

_____

_____

_____

_____

_____

_____

Daily Affirmation about myself

I AM:

Happiness Scale % :

0   25   50   75   100

Storms don't last forever

Daily Gratitude

DATE:

I am grateful for:

_____

_____

_____

_____

_____

_____

_____

_____

_____

_____

_____

_____

_____

_____

_____

_____

_____

_____

Daily Affirmation about myself

I AM:

Happiness Scale % :

0   25   50   75   100

What consumes your mind consumes your life

Daily Gratitude

DATE:

I am grateful for:

_____

_____

_____

_____

_____

_____

_____

_____

_____

_____

_____

_____

_____

_____

_____

_____

_____

_____

Daily Affirmation about myself
I AM:

Happiness Scale % :

0   25   50   75   100

Reset, re-adjust, re-start, re-focus, as many times as you need

Daily Gratitude

DATE:

I am grateful for:

_____

_____

_____

_____

_____

_____

_____

_____

_____

_____

_____

_____

_____

_____

_____

_____

_____

_____

_____

Daily Affirmation about myself
I AM:

Happiness Scale % :

0   25   50   75   100

The best project you'll ever work on is you. - Sonny Franco

Daily Gratitude

DATE:

I am grateful for:

_____

_____

_____

_____

_____

_____

_____

_____

_____

_____

_____

_____

_____

_____

_____

_____

_____

_____

Daily Affirmation about myself

I AM:

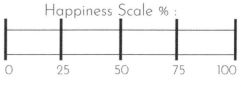

Happiness Scale % :

0   25   50   75   100

Never be afraid to try new things

Daily Gratitude

DATE :

I am grateful for:

_____

_____

_____

_____

_____

_____

_____

_____

_____

_____

_____

_____

_____

_____

_____

_____

_____

_____

_____

Daily Affirmation about myself
I AM:

Happiness Scale % :

0   25   50   75   100

Weekly Reflection

WEEK 24

Write about the 24th week of gratitude and reflect on what you noticed, felt, heard, saw and any other things you may of noticed.

_____

_____

_____

_____

_____

_____

_____

_____

_____

_____

_____

_____

_____

_____

_____

_____

_____

_____

_____

_____

_____

_____

_____

_____

_____

"I love those who can smile in trouble." Leonardo da Vinci

Week 25

Challenge

CELEBRATE:

Take the time to celebrate all your wins BIG or SMALL. It is important to celebrate you!

STOP

S - STOP
T - TAKE A BREATHE
O - OPEN AND OBSERVE
P - PROCEED MINDFULLY

This is to remind you to take the time to STOP. REFOCUS. TAKE A STEP BACK.
Open yourself to a moment - take the time to observe and acknowledge your
thoughts and emotions, then take the time to focus on the here and now. This will
help with cultivating mindfulness.

Take the time to go back to this acronym from time to time, when you are feeling
overwhelmed, stressed, negative or even just to check in throughout the day! Place
reminders around the house - post it notes on the fridge, in the bath room, on the
back of the front door, or home office. It is a great way to STOP and take the time
to check in with you!

RECORD ONE EXPERIENCE HERE BELOW:

_____

_____

_____

_____

_____

_____

_____

_____

_____

_____

_____

_____

_____

_____

_____

_____

_____

Champions believe in themselves even when no one else does

Daily Gratitude

DATE:

I am grateful for:

_____

_____

_____

_____

_____

_____

_____

_____

_____

_____

_____

_____

_____

_____

_____

_____

_____

_____

_____

Daily Affirmation about myself
I AM:

Happiness Scale % :

0   25   50   75   100

Build a life you don't need a vacation from

Daily Gratitude

DATE:

I am grateful for:

_____

_____

_____

_____

_____

_____

_____

_____

_____

_____

_____

_____

_____

_____

_____

_____

_____

_____

_____

_____

_____

Daily Affirmation about myself

I AM:

Happiness Scale % :

0   25   50   75   100

Set a goal that makes you want to jump out of bed in the morning

Daily Gratitude

DATE:

I am grateful for:

_____

_____

_____

_____

_____

_____

_____

_____

_____

_____

_____

_____

_____

_____

_____

_____

_____

_____

Daily Affirmation about myself
I AM:

Happiness Scale % :

0   25   50   75   100

Don't look back, you're not going that way. - Mary Engelbreit

Daily Gratitude

DATE:

I am grateful for:

_____

_____

_____

_____

_____

_____

_____

_____

_____

_____

_____

_____

_____

_____

_____

_____

_____

Daily Affirmation about myself

I AM:

Happiness Scale % :

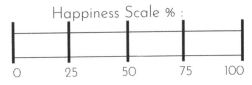

0   25   50   75   100

A person who feels appreciated will always do more than what is expected

Daily Gratitude

DATE:

I am grateful for:

Daily Affirmation about myself
I AM:

Happiness Scale % :

0　　　　25　　　　50　　　　75　　　　100

Dream BIG. Stop thinking small

Daily Gratitude

DATE:

I am grateful for:

_____

_____

_____

_____

_____

_____

_____

_____

_____

_____

_____

_____

_____

_____

_____

_____

_____

Daily Affirmation about myself

I AM:

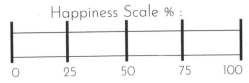

Happiness Scale % :

0   25   50   75   100

Don't tell people your dreams. Show them!

Daily Gratitude

DATE:

I am grateful for:

_____

_____

_____

_____

_____

_____

_____

_____

_____

_____

_____

_____

_____

_____

_____

_____

_____

_____

_____

Daily Affirmation about myself
I AM:

Happiness Scale % :

0   25   50   75   100

Date:

Weekly Reflection

WEEK 25

Write about the 25th week of gratitude and reflect on what you noticed, felt, heard, saw and any other things you may of noticed.

_____

_____

_____

_____

_____

_____

_____

_____

_____

_____

_____

_____

_____

_____

_____

_____

_____

_____

_____

_____

_____

_____

_____

_____

"A disciplined mind
brings happiness."
Buddha

Week 26

Challenge

LETTER:

Write a letter to a friend and post it.

Sunrise

Take some time out for the day and go to bed early, so you can wake up early and watch a sunrise. The beauty, the colours, the sun rising, the birds chirping, the animals waking from sleep it is amazing to notice. Go to the beach or a place where you can watch this in nature.

This is one of the greatest times of the day! The break of day! The new day! The start of something new!

Take a journal or write below about what comes up and what you see, feel, hear:

_____

_____

_____

_____

_____

_____

_____

_____

_____

_____

_____

_____

_____

Tough time never last but tough people do....-Robert H. Schuller

Daily Gratitude

DATE:

I am grateful for:

_____

_____

_____

_____

_____

_____

_____

_____

_____

_____

_____

_____

_____

_____

_____

_____

_____

_____

Daily Affirmation about myself

I AM:

Happiness Scale % :

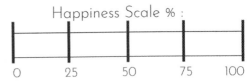

0   25   50   75   100

Check in: Values, boundaries, standards. What's yours?

Daily Gratitude

DATE:

I am grateful for:

_____

_____

_____

_____

_____

_____

_____

_____

_____

_____

_____

_____

_____

_____

_____

_____

_____

_____

_____

_____

Daily Affirmation about myself
I AM:

Happiness Scale % :

0   25   50   75   100

You choose your emotions and reactions to events. Choose the best reaction.

Daily Gratitude

DATE:

I am grateful for:

_____

_____

_____

_____

_____

_____

_____

_____

_____

_____

_____

_____

_____

_____

_____

_____

Daily Affirmation about myself
I AM:

Happiness Scale % :

0   25   50   75   100

Daily Gratitude

DATE:

I am grateful for:

_____

_____

_____

_____

_____

_____

_____

_____

_____

_____

_____

_____

_____

_____

_____

_____

_____

_____

_____

_____

_____

Daily Affirmation about myself
I AM:

Happiness Scale % :

0	25	50	75	100

Pay it forward today

Daily Gratitude

DATE:

I am grateful for:

_____

_____

_____

_____

_____

_____

_____

_____

_____

_____

_____

_____

_____

_____

_____

_____

_____

_____

_____

Daily Affirmation about myself

I AM:

Happiness Scale % :

0   25   50   75   100

Your body is your temple, treat it right

Daily Gratitude

DATE:

I am grateful for:

_____

_____

_____

_____

_____

_____

_____

_____

_____

_____

_____

_____

_____

_____

_____

_____

_____

_____

Daily Affirmation about myself
I AM:

Happiness Scale % :

0   25   50   75   100

Speak your truth and your world will open more. - Alicia Wade

Daily Gratitude

DATE:

I am grateful for:

_____

_____

_____

_____

_____

_____

_____

_____

_____

_____

_____

_____

_____

_____

_____

_____

_____

_____

_____

Daily Affirmation about myself

I AM:

Happiness Scale % :

0   25   50   75   100

Date:

Weekly Reflection

Write about the 26th week of gratitude and reflect on what you noticed, felt, heard, saw and any other things you may of noticed.

"Look back and be grateful, look ahead and be hopeful, look around and be helpful."

Thank you

This page is a dedication page to all my mentors,
all my supporters,
all the people who believed in me to grow.

Pk Savy for always being in that corner whether it be a little message, comment or catch ups! You have seen me grow right from the start! I am so fortunate to be having this journey with you and thank you for being awesome! Thank you for reminding me to be grounded and give WOW!

Daniel Burgess for being the one in my corner backing me up, cheering me in every aspect. Taking me to the next level! Inspiring me to model off the best of the best. I learn so much and love your journey and so honoured to be in this thing called life together xxx

Matt Lavars for his ongoing care, love and support to my journey. The guidance and wisdom he brings to show up only assists me with being the best I can be! Thank you for always inspiring me!

Ilsé Strauss for being an amazing leadership coach and stretching me in every hot seat - maybe third time round we can see my face! Thank you for your ongoing support and love!

Sharon Pearson for the Coaching Institute, this has enable me to do the things I am doing today! A published author! Who would have thought!

Thank you

Teash Ology for your loving comments and feedback and quick comments! I truly appreciate the support you give to me and the community you are phenomenal at what you do!

Joe Pane for all the interviews I've had recently and allowing me to be a part of your FOCs training's. I've learnt a lot from you as a facilitator. I love your kindness and warmth you bring.

Sohret Hussein your ongoing support love and care to my world, you are one of my soul sisters and I love having a connection with you.

Fatima Raad there is never a dull day with you. You can always help me through my shit and then put a smile after I have released whatever shit I am holding onto. Thank you for always being a champion!

Matt Patterson for always being there for me emotionally, I feel we are so in tune with our journey and I have to say the last two weeks you have been so kind to give space and I know I do this for you too. You are a amazing human.

Hayley Latcham my pommie pocket rocket! I love you and all you bring to this journey and the high vibe, passion you bring to your arena, the inspiration you bring to my life daily!

Hazel Vertley my ying and I am your yang. We are soul sisters. I love you forever and always!

Thank you

I want to take the time to personally thank you for your support, your involvement with my gratitude journey as I create another version of this book. Each time a book is purchased I know I have touched another person's heart.

I know people love this,

I know cultivating Gratitude works

know when we bring this in it changes your perspective.

It's time to change and ACT NOW!

Visit:

www.hbgratitude.com.au

Thank you and enjoy your continuing journey to happiness and Gratitude.

Because Gratitude is the best attitude!

Alicia Ann Wade
Gratitude Expert, Coach, Mentor, Key Note Speaker & Author

Printed in the United States
by Baker & Taylor Publisher Services